Travel Guide

To

Bayeux

Explore the Heart of Normandy with Tips on When to visit, How to prepare and Detailed Itineraries for a wonderful Experience

Bryan J. Zehner

Copyright© 2024 Bryan J. Zehner. All rights reserved. No part of this publication may be reproduced, distributed, or transmitted in any form without the prior written permission of the publisher.

Disclaimer: *The information, contacts, websites, and costs provided in this book were accurate at the time of publication. Readers are advised to verify current details as information may have changed since publication.*

Content

Introduction 6
Chapter 1 14
   Getting to Bayeux 14
      Travel Options (By Air, Train, Car) 14
      Local Transportation (Buses, Taxis, Biking) 18
Chapter 2 23
   Where to Stay 23
      Top Hotels 23
      Budget Accommodations 28
      Unique Stays (B&Bs, Historical Inns) 31
Chapter 3 37
   Exploring the Bayeux Tapestry 37
      History and Significance 37
      Tips for a Great Visit 42
Chapter 4 47
   Historical Sites and Museums 47
      Bayeux Cathedral 47
      The Battle of Normandy Museum 50
      Other Notable Museums and Sites 52
Chapter 5 58
   Outdoor Activities and Natural Attractions 58
      Botanical Gardens 58
      Walking and Cycling Routes 60
      Parks and Picnic Spots 64
Chapter 6 68

Food and Dining.. 68
   Traditional Norman Cuisine..68
   Top Restaurants and Cafés... 70
   Food Markets and Local Specialties........................ 72

Chapter 7.. **75**
  Shopping in Bayeux.. 75
   Souvenir Shops.. 75
   Local Markets.. 77

Chapter 8.. **80**
  Day Trips and Excursions...80
   D-Day Landing Beaches... 80
   Nearby Villages and Towns.. 84
   Scenic Drives and Tours... 87

Chapter 9.. **90**
  Cultural Events and Festivals... 90
   Annual Festivals and Events.....................................90
   Theater and Performances..93
   Local Traditions and Celebrations........................... 95
   7 Days Itinerary..97

Chapter 10.. **101**
  Practical Information... 101
   Tourist Information Centers..................................... 101
   Emergency Contacts... 103
   Hospitals and Medical Services.............................. 104
   Pharmacies.. 105
   Travel Tips and Safety Advice.................................105
   Visa Requirement and Permit.................................. 107
   Work and Study Permits.. 109

Conclusion..**111**
Bonus.. **114**

Introduction

Bayeux is a charming town located in the Normandy region of northwestern France. Known for its picturesque medieval architecture, cobblestone streets, and rich cultural heritage, Bayeux offers a delightful blend of history and modern-day attractions. Situated near the D-Day landing beaches, it serves as an essential stop for visitors interested in World War II history. The town is also famous for the Bayeux Tapestry, a remarkable piece of medieval art that depicts the events leading up to the Norman conquest of England.

The town itself is small and easily navigable on foot, allowing visitors to immerse themselves in its quaint atmosphere. Strolling through Bayeux, one can appreciate the well-preserved buildings, charming shops, and cozy cafés that line its streets. The River

Aure runs through the town, adding to its picturesque charm and providing scenic spots for relaxation.

Bayeux is more than just a historical relic; it is a vibrant town with a thriving community. The local market, held weekly, offers a chance to experience the flavors and products of the region. Fresh produce, cheese, seafood, and other local specialties can be found here, providing a taste of Normandy's culinary delights. The town's restaurants and bistros offer a mix of traditional Norman dishes and contemporary cuisine, ensuring that there is something to satisfy every palate.

Accommodation in Bayeux ranges from luxurious hotels to charming bed and breakfasts, catering to a variety of preferences and budgets. Many of these establishments are housed in historic buildings, offering a unique and authentic experience for visitors. The town is also known for its hospitality, with friendly locals who are eager to share their knowledge and love of the area with travelers.

Bayeux's strategic location makes it an ideal base for exploring the broader region of Normandy. The D-Day landing beaches are just a short drive away, allowing visitors to delve into the history of World War II and pay tribute to the soldiers who fought there. The nearby towns and villages, each with their own unique charm, are also worth exploring. From the picturesque port town of Honfleur to the imposing Mont Saint-Michel, Normandy offers a wealth of attractions within easy reach of Bayeux.

The town also hosts several cultural events and festivals throughout the year, adding to its appeal. The annual Medieval Festival of Bayeux is a highlight, transforming the town into a lively medieval market with performances, parades, and reenactments. Other events, such as the Bayeux War Correspondents' Awards, attract visitors and highlight the town's ongoing relevance in contemporary culture.

Bayeux holds a significant place in history, primarily due to its connection to the Norman conquest of England and its role in World War II. The Bayeux Tapestry, a masterpiece of medieval embroidery, is one of the most important artifacts associated with the town. This remarkable work of art, nearly 70 meters long, depicts the events leading up to the Battle of Hastings in 1066, where William the Conqueror, Duke of Normandy, defeated King Harold II of England. The tapestry is not only a stunning piece of craftsmanship but also a vital historical document, providing insight into the events and culture of the time.

The Bayeux Tapestry is believed to have been commissioned by Bishop Odo, William the Conqueror's half-brother, and it was likely created in England in the 11th century. It has survived the centuries remarkably well and is now housed in the Bayeux Museum, where it attracts visitors from around the world. The tapestry's detailed and vivid scenes offer a unique glimpse into the medieval world, portraying everything from the construction of ships to the brutal realities of battle.

Bayeux's significance extends beyond the Norman conquest. During World War II, the town played a crucial role in the Allied invasion of Normandy. On June 6, 1944, known as D-Day, Allied forces landed on the beaches of Normandy, marking the beginning of the end of Nazi occupation in Western Europe. Bayeux was one of the first towns to be liberated by the Allies, and it quickly became a center of operations for the British forces.

The liberation of Bayeux was relatively peaceful, with the town spared the extensive damage suffered by many other Normandy towns and cities. This has allowed Bayeux to retain much of its historic architecture, offering visitors a rare glimpse of a medieval town that has remained largely intact. The Bayeux War Cemetery, located just outside the town, is the largest Commonwealth cemetery in France, and it serves as a poignant reminder of the sacrifices made during the liberation of Europe.

Bayeux also hosts the Bayeux War Correspondents' Memorial, which honors journalists who have lost their lives in conflicts around the world. This memorial underscores the town's ongoing connection to the theme of liberation and its commitment to remembering the past while engaging with contemporary issues.

The town's cathedral, Notre-Dame de Bayeux, is another significant historical site. In the presence of William the Conqueror, this magnificent Gothic building was dedicated in 1077. The cathedral has undergone several modifications over the centuries, but it remains a stunning example of medieval architecture. Its grandeur and historical importance make it a key attraction for visitors to Bayeux.

Throughout its history, Bayeux has managed to preserve its heritage while adapting to the changing times. Its role in significant historical events, from the Norman conquest to World War II, has left an indelible mark on the town. Today, Bayeux stands as a proof to resilience and continuity, offering visitors a chance to explore and reflect on its rich past.

Chapter 1

Getting to Bayeux

Travel Options (By Air, Train, Car)

Bayeux, located in the Normandy region of France, is accessible through various modes of transportation, making it a convenient destination for travelers. Understanding the different travel options and associated costs can help in planning a seamless journey to this historical town.

By Air

The nearest major airport to Bayeux is Caen-Carpiquet Airport (CFR), situated approximately 30 kilometers (about 18.6 miles) from Bayeux. This regional airport handles flights from several European cities, including Paris, Lyon, and Marseille, among others. For international travelers, Paris Charles de Gaulle Airport (CDG) and Paris Orly Airport (ORY) are the most common entry points, both located about 260 kilometers (approximately 162 miles) from Bayeux.

Flight Costs:
- Flights from London to Caen-Carpiquet Airport typically range from €100 to €200 for a round trip, depending on the season and airline.
- International flights to Paris from major cities like New York, London, or Berlin can range from €400 to €800 for a round trip.

From Paris, travelers can take a train or drive to Bayeux. Alternatively, there are car rental services available at both Paris and Caen airports.

By Train

France boasts an extensive and efficient train network, making travel by train a popular choice for reaching Bayeux. The Bayeux train station (Gare de Bayeux) is well-connected, with regular services from Paris and other major cities.

Train Routes and Costs:

- From Paris: The direct train from Paris Saint-Lazare to Bayeux takes approximately 2 hours and 15 minutes. The ticket price for a one-way trip ranges from €15 to €50, depending on the time of booking and class of service.

- From Caen: A regional train from Caen to Bayeux takes about 20 minutes, with ticket prices ranging from €5 to €10.

For schedules and booking, travelers can visit the SNCF website (https://www.sncf.com) or contact the SNCF customer service at +33 8 92 35 35 35.

By Car

Traveling to Bayeux by car offers flexibility and the opportunity to explore the scenic routes of Normandy.

Driving Directions:
- From Paris: Take the A13 motorway towards Caen, then the N13 road to Bayeux. The journey takes approximately 3 hours, covering around 270 kilometers (about 168 miles).
- From Caen: Take the N13 road directly to Bayeux, a 30-minute drive over approximately 30 kilometers (about 18.6 miles).

Car Rental Costs:

- Car rental prices vary depending on the vehicle type and rental duration. On average, daily rental rates range from €30 to €100.

-Major car rental agencies include Hertz (https://www.hertz.com),Avis(https://www.avis.com), and Europcar (https://www.europcar.com).

Parking in Bayeux is relatively easy, with several public parking lots available. Visitors can also inquire about parking options at their accommodations.

Local Transportation (Buses, Taxis, Biking)

Once in Bayeux, getting around the town and exploring nearby attractions is straightforward, thanks to a variety of local transportation options.

Buses

Bayeux has a reliable and affordable local bus service operated by the regional transport network, Bus Verts du Calvados. Buses connect the town with surrounding areas, including Caen and the D-Day landing beaches.

Bus Costs:

- A single ticket within Bayeux costs around €1.50.
- Day passes are available for €4.50, offering unlimited travel on the local bus network.

For schedules, routes, and additional information, travelers can visit the Bus Verts du Calvados website (https://www.busverts.fr) or call their customer service at +33 2 31 15 55 55.

Taxis

Taxis are readily available in Bayeux and can be a convenient option for short trips or when traveling with luggage. Taxi ranks are located at key points such as the train station and main squares.

Taxi Costs:

- The initial fare is approximately €2.50, with additional charges of around €1.50 per kilometer.
- A typical trip within Bayeux costs between €10 and €20, depending on distance and time of day.

Travelers can book a taxi in advance by calling local taxi services such as Taxis Bayeusains at +33 6 09 66 35 35.

Biking

Bayeux is a bike-friendly town with several rental options for those who prefer cycling. Biking is an excellent way to explore the town at a leisurely pace and visit nearby sites.

Bike Rental Costs:

- Daily bike rental rates range from €10 to €20.
- Weekly rentals are available, typically costing between €50 and €100.

Several local shops offer bike rentals, including Bayeux Bike Hire, which can be contacted at +33 61 513 67 86.

Biking Routes:

- Bayeux offers dedicated cycling paths and scenic routes through the countryside.
- Popular routes include rides to the D-Day landing beaches and along the Aure River.

Chapter 2

Where to Stay

Top Hotels

Hotel Villa Lara

Located in the heart of Bayeux, Hotel Villa Lara is a boutique hotel known for its elegance and exceptional service. It offers a blend of traditional charm and modern amenities, making it a preferred choice for discerning travelers.

Cost per Night:
- Prices range from €200 to €350, depending on the room type and season.

Address:

- No. 6 Place du Québec, 14400 Bayeux, France

Phone Contact:

- +33 2 31 92 00 55

Website:

- (https://www.hotel-villalara.com)

Hotel Villa Lara features 28 individually decorated rooms and suites, all offering stunning views of the Bayeux Cathedral or the hotel's beautiful garden. Each room is equipped with high-end amenities, including free Wi-Fi, flat-screen TVs, and luxurious toiletries. Guests can enjoy a gourmet breakfast in the charming dining room or relax with a drink in the elegant bar. The hotel's central location makes it an ideal base for exploring Bayeux's historical sites and nearby attractions.

Château La Chenevière

For those seeking a luxurious countryside retreat, Château La Chenevière offers an unforgettable stay. This 18th-century château combines historic charm with modern luxury, set within a sprawling park.

Cost per Night:
- Prices range from €250 to €500, depending on the room type and season.

Address:
- Escures-Commes, 14520 Port-en-Bessin-Huppain, France

Phone Contact:
- +33 2 31 51 25 25

Website:

- (https://www.lacheneviere.com)

Château La Chenevière features elegantly furnished rooms and suites, each uniquely decorated and offering views of the garden or park. The hotel boasts an outdoor heated pool, a tennis court, and a gourmet restaurant that serves refined French cuisine using locally sourced ingredients. Guests can also enjoy activities such as cycling and golf in the surrounding area. The château's proximity to the D-Day landing beaches and other historical sites makes it a perfect destination for history enthusiasts.

Hotel Churchill

Hotel Churchill is another excellent choice for travelers who value both comfort and location. Situated just steps away from the Bayeux Tapestry Museum, this hotel is known for its warm hospitality and cozy ambiance.

Cost per Night:

- Prices range from €100 to €200, depending on the room type and season.

Address:

- 14-16 Rue Saint-Jean, 14400 Bayeux, France

Phone Contact:

- +33 2 31 21 31 80

Website:

- (https://www.hotel-churchill.fr)

Hotel Churchill offers well-appointed rooms with modern amenities such as free Wi-Fi, flat-screen TVs, and air conditioning. The hotel also features a charming lounge where guests can relax after a day of sightseeing. Its central location provides easy access to Bayeux's main attractions, including the

Bayeux Cathedral and the Battle of Normandy Museum.

Budget Accommodations

Ibis Budget Bayeux

Ibis Budget Bayeux is a popular choice for budget-conscious travelers seeking clean and comfortable accommodations. This hotel offers excellent value for money, with modern amenities and friendly service.

Cost per Night:
- Prices range from €50 to €80, depending on the room type and season.

Address:

- ZA Nonant, 14400 Bayeux, France

Phone Contact:
- +33 8 92 68 32 41

Website:
- (https://www.accorhotels.com)

Ibis Budget Bayeux features simple yet comfortable rooms equipped with free Wi-Fi, flat-screen TVs, and air conditioning. The hotel offers a continental breakfast buffet and free parking, making it a convenient option for travelers with rental cars. Its location just outside the city center provides easy access to Bayeux's attractions and the surrounding countryside.

Premiere Classe Bayeux

Another budget-friendly option is Premiere Classe Bayeux, offering basic yet comfortable accommodations at an affordable price.

Cost per Night:

- Prices range from €40 to €70, depending on the room type and season.

Address:

- Chemin de la Gambette, 14400 Bayeux, France

Phone Contact:

- +33 2 31 10 13 30

Website:

- (https://www.premiereclasse.com)

Premiere Classe Bayeux offers compact rooms with essential amenities such as free Wi-Fi, flat-screen TVs, and en-suite bathrooms. The hotel provides a breakfast buffet and free parking. Its location near the Bayeux train station and major attractions makes it a convenient base for exploring the town and nearby sites.

Unique Stays (B&Bs, Historical Inns)

For a more personalized and unique experience, consider staying at one of Bayeux's charming bed and breakfasts or historical inns. These accommodations often provide a more intimate atmosphere and a taste of local hospitality.

Le Manoir Sainte Victoire

Le Manoir Sainte Victoire is a beautiful bed and breakfast set in a historic building in the heart of Bayeux. It offers a unique blend of old-world charm and modern comfort.

Cost per Night:

- Prices range from €120 to €180, depending on the room type and season.

Address:

- 32, rue de la Juridiction 14400 BAYEUX

Phone Contact:

Tél : 02 31 22 74 69

Mobile : 06 85 02 67 97

Email : contact@manoirsaintevictoire.com

Website:

- (https://www.manoirsaintevictoire.com/)

www.manoirsaintevictoire.com

contact@manoirsaintevictoire.com

Le Manoir Sainte Victoire features elegantly furnished rooms with antique decor and modern amenities such as free Wi-Fi, flat-screen TVs, and private bathrooms. Guests can enjoy a delicious homemade breakfast each morning and relax in the lovely garden. The bed and breakfast's central location allows easy access to Bayeux's main attractions, including the Bayeux Tapestry Museum and the Bayeux Cathedral.

Hôtel d'Argouges

Hôtel d'Argouges is a historical inn located in a charming 18th-century townhouse. This hotel offers a unique blend of history, elegance, and modern comfort, making it a memorable place to stay.

Cost per Night:

- Prices range from €100 to €200, depending on the room type and season.

Address:
- 21 Rue Saint-Patrice, 14400 Bayeux, France

Phone Contact:
- +33 2 31 92 88 86

Hôtel d'Argouges features beautifully decorated rooms with period furnishings and modern amenities such as free Wi-Fi, flat-screen TVs, and air conditioning. Guests can enjoy a delightful breakfast in the elegant dining room or on the terrace overlooking the garden. The inn's central location makes it easy to explore Bayeux's historical sites and enjoy the town's vibrant atmosphere.

La Ferme de la Gronde

For a truly unique stay, consider La Ferme de la Gronde, a charming bed and breakfast located on a working farm just outside Bayeux.

Cost per Night:
- Prices range from €80 to €150, depending on the room type and season.

Address:
- Le Bourg, 14400 Magny-en-Bessin, France

Phone Contact:
- +33 2 31 21 33 11

Website:
-(https://recorriendomundos.com/france/magny-en-bessin/la-ferme-de-la-gronde/)

La Ferme de la Gronde features cozy rooms and cottages with rustic decor and modern amenities such as free Wi-Fi and private bathrooms. Guests can enjoy a hearty farmhouse breakfast each morning and explore the beautiful countryside surrounding the farm. The bed and breakfast is located just a short drive from Bayeux, making it a convenient base for exploring the town and the Normandy region.

Chapter 3

Exploring the Bayeux Tapestry

The Bayeux Tapestry is one of the most significant and well-preserved artifacts from the medieval period. It offers a unique glimpse into the events leading up to the Norman conquest of England in 1066.

History and Significance

The Bayeux Tapestry as explained in the Introductory part earlier is actually an embroidered cloth, approximately 70 meters long and 50 centimeters tall. It vividly depicts the events leading up to the Battle of Hastings in 1066 and the subsequent Norman conquest of England. The tapestry is divided into 58 scenes, each meticulously detailed with figures, animals, and inscriptions in Latin.

The creation of the tapestry is attributed to Bishop Odo of Bayeux, the half-brother of William the Conqueror. It is believed to have been made in the 1070s, probably in England, due to the stylistic elements that match other Anglo-Saxon art from the period. The primary purpose of the tapestry was likely to celebrate William's victory and legitimate his claim to the English throne. It also served as a tool for educating the largely illiterate population about these pivotal events.

The tapestry's historical significance cannot be overstated. It provides invaluable insights into the armor, weapons, ships, and everyday life of the 11th century. The depiction of the Battle of Hastings is particularly detailed, showing tactics, formations, and even individual moments of heroism and tragedy. The tapestry also offers a rare glimpse into the medieval world's social and political landscape, highlighting the power dynamics between different factions.

Beyond its historical value, the Bayeux Tapestry is an extraordinary work of art. The craftsmanship involved in its creation is remarkable, with detailed embroidery using wool yarns of various colors on a linen background. The figures are expressive, the composition is dynamic, and the overall narrative is both engaging and informative.

Visiting the Tapestry Museum

The Bayeux Tapestry is housed in the Bayeux Museum, which is located in the heart of the town of Bayeux, Normandy. The museum itself is situated in the former Seminary of Bayeux, a historic

18th-century building that adds to the charm and atmosphere of the visit.

Entry to the museum costs €9.50 for adults and €5 for students and children under 18. Children under 10 can enter for free, making it an accessible attraction for families. The museum offers discounted rates for groups and provides free entry on the first Sunday of each month from November to March.

The address of the Bayeux Museum is 13B Rue de Nesmond, 14400 Bayeux, France. For inquiries or additional information, you can contact the museum at +33 2 31 51 25 50 or visit their official website at (https://www.bayeuxmuseum.com).

ACCESS BY CAR

From Caen: N13 exit 36 towards Bayeux

From Rennes: A84 or E03 towards Caen exit 43, then D6

ACCESS BY PLANE

Paris Airport, then train access from Saint-Lazare station to Bayeux station

ACCESS BY TRAIN

Bayeux train station

stop Pedestrian journey to the museums takes approximately 10 to 15 minutes

The tapestry is displayed in a specially designed, climate-controlled room to ensure its preservation. Visitors can walk along the length of the tapestry, viewing each panel up close and appreciating the intricate details and craftsmanship. An audio guide, available in several languages, provides a comprehensive explanation of each scene, enhancing the visitor's understanding of the tapestry's narrative.

Tips for a Great Visit

First, arriving early in the day or late in the afternoon can help you avoid the crowds and enjoy a more relaxed experience. The museum can get busy, especially during peak tourist season, so timing your visit can make a significant difference.

Using the audio guide is highly recommended. It provides detailed explanations of each scene depicted in the tapestry, available in multiple languages, helping visitors understand the historical context and significance of the artwork. This adds depth to the experience and ensures that you don't miss any important details.

Allowing enough time for your visit is also important. While the tapestry itself can be viewed in about an hour, it's worth spending additional time exploring the other exhibits in the museum. The information provided on the history and preservation of the tapestry is fascinating and adds depth to your understanding.

Visiting the museum's gift shop can be a delightful way to end your tour. The shop offers a range of souvenirs, books, and replicas related to the Bayeux Tapestry. It's a great place to pick up a memento of your visit.

After visiting the museum, take some time to explore the charming town of Bayeux. The Bayeux Cathedral, just a short walk from the museum, is another historical gem worth visiting. The town itself is picturesque, with quaint streets, traditional

Norman architecture, and a variety of cafes and restaurants where you can relax and enjoy the local cuisine.

For accommodation, there are several excellent options nearby. Hotel Villa Lara, located at 6 Place du Québec, offers luxurious rooms with rates ranging from €200 to €350 per night. You can contact them at +33 2 31 92 00 55 or visit their website at (https://www.hotel-villalara.com). For a more budget-friendly option, consider Ibis Budget Bayeux, located at ZA Nonant, with rates from €50 to €80 per night. Their contact number is +33 8 92 68 32 41, and their website is (https://www.accorhotels.com).

Getting to the Bayeux Tapestry Museum is convenient, with several transportation options available. If you're arriving by air, the nearest major airport is Caen Carpiquet Airport (CFR), located about 30 kilometers from Bayeux. From the airport, you can take a taxi or rent a car to reach Bayeux. The town is well-connected by train, with regular services from Paris, Caen, and other major cities. The Bayeux train station is about a 15-minute walk from the museum. Bayeux is easily accessible by car, with well-marked roads leading into the town, and ample parking available near the museum. Local buses also serve Bayeux, providing convenient connections to nearby towns and attractions.

Visiting the Bayeux Tapestry is a highlight for many travelers to Normandy. Its historical significance, artistic beauty, and the fascinating story it tells make it a must-see attraction. By planning your visit carefully and taking advantage of the resources available at the museum, you can have an enriching and memorable experience exploring this medieval masterpiece.

Chapter 4

Historical Sites and Museums

Bayeux Cathedral

Bayeux Cathedral, officially known as the Cathedral of Our Lady of Bayeux, is a stunning example of Norman architecture. Built in the 11th century, it is a masterpiece of medieval construction, with its towering spires and intricate details. The cathedral was consecrated in 1077 in the presence of William the Conqueror and served as the original home of the Bayeux Tapestry before it was moved to its current location.

The cathedral's architecture is a blend of Romanesque and Gothic styles, reflecting its construction and renovation phases over the centuries. The interior is equally impressive, with its soaring vaulted ceilings, beautiful stained glass windows, and detailed carvings. One of the most striking features is the crypt, which dates back to the 11th century and contains well-preserved frescoes that offer a glimpse into the art and religious practices of the time.

Entry to Bayeux Cathedral is free, making it an accessible attraction for all visitors. Guided tours are available for those interested in learning more about the cathedral's history, architecture, and significance. The cathedral is located at 13 Rue de Nesmond, 14400 Bayeux, France. For more information, you can contact the cathedral at +33 2 31920185 or visit (https://www.bayeux.fr/fr/decouvrir-bayeux/cathedrale-notre-dame).

Nearby accommodations include the Hotel Reine Mathilde, located at 23 Rue Larcher, offering rooms from €80 to €150 per night. You can contact them at +33 2 31 92 08 13 or visit their website at (https://hotel-bayeux-reinemathilde.fr/). Another excellent option is the Churchill Hotel, located at 14-16 Rue Saint-Jean, with rates ranging from €100 to €200 per night. Their contact number is +33 2 31 21 31 80, and their website is (https://www.hotel-churchill.fr).

Reaching the cathedral is straightforward. If you're arriving by train, the Bayeux train station is about a 15-minute walk away. For those driving, there are several parking lots nearby, including one directly in front of the cathedral. Local buses also stop near the cathedral, making it easily accessible by public transport.

The Battle of Normandy Museum

The Battle of Normandy Museum is dedicated to the events of D-Day and the subsequent Battle of Normandy in 1944. This museum offers a detailed and moving account of one of the most significant military operations in history, highlighting the bravery and sacrifice of those involved.

The museum's exhibits include a wide range of artifacts, such as uniforms, weapons, maps, and photographs. There are also detailed dioramas and multimedia presentations that help bring the events of the battle to life. One of the highlights is the large-scale map showing the movements of the Allied and German forces during the battle, providing a comprehensive overview of the campaign.

The museum also features a memorial garden, where visitors can reflect on the sacrifices made during the battle. The garden includes plaques and monuments dedicated to the soldiers from various nations who fought and died in Normandy.

Entry to the Battle of Normandy Museum costs €7.50 for adults and €4.50 for students and children. Children under 10 can enter for free. The museum is located at Boulevard Fabian Ware, 14400 Bayeux, France. For more information, you can contact the museum at +33231514690 or visit (https://www.musee-memorial-omaha.com).

For accommodation, consider staying at the Hotel Le Bayeux, located at 9 Rue Tardif, with room rates from €70 to €120 per night. You can contact them at +33 2 31 92 70 08 or visit their website at (https://www.hotellebayeux.com/). Another nearby option is the Novotel Bayeux, located at 117 Rue

Saint-Patrice, with rates ranging from €100 to €180 per night. Their contact number is +33231921611, and their website is (https://all.accor.com/hotel/0964/index.en.shtml?utm_campaign=seo+maps&utm_medium=seo+maps&utm_source=google+Maps).

The museum is about a 20-minute walk from the Bayeux train station. Local buses also serve the area, providing easy access for those using public transport.

Other Notable Museums and Sites

The Baron Gérard Museum of Art and History, also known as the MAHB (Musée d'Art et d'Histoire Baron Gérard), is housed in the former Bishop's Palace, a historic building in the heart of Bayeux. The museum's collection spans from prehistory to the 20th century, with exhibits including paintings, sculptures, ceramics, and archaeological artifacts. Entry to the MAHB costs €7.50 for adults and €4 for students and children. The museum is located at 37 Rue du Bienvenu, 14400 Bayeux, France. For more information, you can contact them at +33 2 31 92 14 21 or visit (https://www.bayeuxmuseum.com/).

For accommodation near the MAHB, consider the Hôtel d'Argouges, located at 21 Rue Saint-Patrice, with rates from €90 to €150 per night. You can contact them at +33 2 31 92 88 86. Another nearby option is the Hotel Le Lion d'Or, located at 71 Rue Saint-Jean, with rates ranging from €100 to €200 per night. Their contact number is +33 2 31 92 06 90, and their website is (https://www.liondor-bayeux.fr).

Another must-visit site is the British War Cemetery, the largest Commonwealth cemetery in Normandy, where nearly 5,000 soldiers are buried. The cemetery is a poignant reminder of the sacrifices made during the Battle of Normandy and is meticulously maintained. The cemetery is open to the public free of charge and is located at Boulevard Fabian Ware, 14400 Bayeux, France. For more information, you can contact the Commonwealth War Graves Commission at +44 1628 507200 or visit their website at (https://www.cwgc.org).

For those interested in more recent history, the Radar Museum is a fascinating attraction dedicated to the technology and use of radar during World War II. Located in the nearby town of Douvres-la-Délivrande, about 20 kilometers from Bayeux, the museum is housed in a former German radar station. Entry to the Radar Museum costs €7 for adults and €5 for children. The address is Route de Bény, 14440 Douvres-la-Délivrande, France. For more information, you can contact the museum at

+33 2 31 37 32 86 or visit their website at (https://www.musee-radar.fr).

Nearby accommodations include the Hotel de la Gare, located at 2 Avenue de la Gare, with room rates from €60 to €100 per night. You can contact them at +33 2 31 37 25 50. Another option is the Kyriad Direct Caen Nord - Memorial, Kyriad Direct Caen Nord – Memorial

Address
5 Rue Du Clos Barbey
14280 Saint Contest, France
See itineraries

Booking :
+33 1 73 21 98 00
7 days a week from 8:00 a.m. to 22:00 p.m. (Paris time) - Cost of a local call

Call the hotel : +33 2 31073550 and their website is (https://direct-caen-nord-memorial.kyriad.com/en-us/).

To reach these historical sites and museums, visitors can use various transportation options. Bayeux is well-connected by train, with regular services from major cities such as Paris and Caen. The town is also easily accessible by car, with several parking facilities available near the main attractions. Local buses provide convenient connections within Bayeux and to nearby towns, making it easy to explore the region without a car. Taxis and bike rentals are also available for those who prefer more flexible transportation options.

Chapter 5

Outdoor Activities and Natural Attractions

Botanical Gardens

The Botanical Gardens of Bayeux, also known as Les Jardins Botaniques de Bayeux, are a haven for plant enthusiasts and those looking to enjoy a tranquil environment. Established in the 19th century, these gardens cover an area of approximately 2.6 hectares and showcase a wide variety of plant species, including rare and exotic plants.

The gardens are divided into several themed sections, each offering a unique experience. Visitors can explore the rose garden, which features a stunning collection of roses in various colors and varieties, or wander through the arboretum, home to a diverse range of trees from around the world. The botanical gardens also include a beautiful pond, providing a serene spot for relaxation and reflection.

Entry to the Botanical Gardens of Bayeux is free, making it an accessible attraction for all visitors. The gardens are located at Boulevard Fabian Ware, 14400 Bayeux, France. For more information, you can contact the gardens at +33 2 31 51 60 60 or visit their official website at (https://www.bayeux.fr/fr/lieu/le-jardin-botanique).

For nearby accommodation, consider the Grand Hôtel du Luxembourg, located at 25 Rue des Bouchers, offering rooms from €100 to €200 per night. You can contact them at +33 2 31 92 00 04 or visit their website at

(https://www.grand-hotel-luxembourg.com/).
Another excellent option is the Hotel de Brunville, located at 9 Rue Genas-DuHomme, with rates ranging from €90 to €160 per night. Their contact number is +33 2 31 92 00 04, and their website is (https://www.hotel-de-brunville.com/).

Reaching the Botanical Gardens is easy. If you are arriving by train, the Bayeux train station is about a 15-minute walk away. Local buses also stop near the gardens, making them easily accessible by public transport.

Walking and Cycling Routes

Bayeux and its surrounding areas offer a variety of walking and cycling routes that cater to all levels of fitness and interest. These routes provide an excellent way to explore the region's natural beauty, historical sites, and charming villages at a leisurely pace.

One of the most popular walking routes is the Circuit des Remparts, a scenic path that takes visitors along the ancient city walls of Bayeux. This route offers stunning views of the town and its surrounding countryside, as well as glimpses of historical landmarks such as the Bayeux Cathedral and the Bayeux Tapestry Museum. The Circuit des Remparts is relatively short and easy, making it suitable for walkers of all ages and abilities.

For those looking for a more challenging hike, the Sentier de la Vallée de l'Aure is an excellent choice. This trail takes hikers through the beautiful Aure Valley, passing by rolling hills, lush forests, and picturesque meadows. Along the way, visitors can enjoy the tranquility of nature and spot local wildlife. The Sentier de la Vallée de l'Aure is well-marked and offers several resting points where hikers can take a break and enjoy the scenery.

Cyclists will find plenty of routes to explore as well. The Vélo Francette is a popular cycling trail that runs through Bayeux, connecting the town to other parts of Normandy and beyond. This route is part of a larger network of cycling paths that stretch from Ouistreham on the Normandy coast to La Rochelle on the Atlantic coast. The Vélo Francette offers a mix of flat and hilly terrain, making it suitable for both casual cyclists and more experienced riders.

For a shorter cycling adventure, the Bayeux to Arromanches route is a great option. This path takes cyclists from Bayeux to the coastal town of Arromanches, passing through scenic countryside and historic sites related to the D-Day landings. The route is relatively flat and well-paved, making it an enjoyable ride for cyclists of all skill levels.

Bike rentals are available in Bayeux for those who do not have their own bicycles. Several rental shops in town offer a variety of bikes, including road bikes, mountain bikes, and electric bikes. One such rental shop is Bayeux Bike Rental, located at 5 Rue Saint-Patrice. They offer bikes for rent starting at €15 per day. You can contact them at +33 2 31 92 78 67 or visit (https://www.cctbikerental.com/rentals/bayeux-bike-rentals/).

For accommodation, consider the Hotel Le Bayeux, located at 9 Rue Tardif, with room rates from €70 to €120 per night. You can contact them at +33 2 31 92 70 08 or visit their website at (https://www.hotellebayeux.com/). Another nearby option is the Novotel Bayeux, located at 117 Rue Saint-Patrice, with rates ranging from €100 to €180 per night. Their contact number is +33 2 31 92 16

11, and their website is (https://all.accor.com/hotel/0964/index.en.shtml?utm_campaign=seo+maps&utm_medium=seo+maps&utm_source=google+Maps).

Getting to these walking and cycling routes is convenient, with many starting points accessible by foot from the center of Bayeux. For longer routes, public transport options such as buses and trains can take you to the starting points, and bike rentals can be arranged in town.

Parks and Picnic Spots

Bayeux offers several parks and picnic spots where visitors can relax and enjoy the natural beauty of the area. These green spaces provide a perfect setting for a leisurely afternoon with family and friends.

One of the most popular parks in Bayeux is Parc Michel d'Ornano, located near the center of town. This spacious park features well-manicured lawns, beautiful flower beds, and a variety of trees, providing plenty of shade on sunny days. The park also has a playground for children, making it a great spot for families. Parc Michel d'Ornano is an ideal place for a picnic, with several benches and picnic tables available for use.

Another lovely picnic spot is the Jardin Public de Bayeux, a smaller but equally charming park located near the Bayeux Tapestry Museum. This park is beautifully landscaped, with a variety of plants and flowers that bloom throughout the year. The Jardin Public de Bayeux offers a peaceful setting for a relaxing afternoon, with plenty of seating areas and open spaces for picnicking.

For those looking to venture a bit further, the Parc Naturel Régional des Marais du Cotentin et du Bessin is a fantastic option. This regional natural park covers a vast area of wetlands, meadows, and forests, offering a diverse range of habitats for wildlife. Visitors can explore the park's numerous walking and cycling trails, go birdwatching, or simply enjoy a picnic in one of the many scenic spots. The park is located about 30 kilometers from Bayeux, and entry is free. For more information, you can contact the park at +33 2 33 71 65 30 or visit their official website at (https://www.parc-cotentin-bessin.fr).

Nearby accommodations include the Château de Bellefontaine, located at 49 Rue de Bellefontaine, with room rates from €120 to €250 per night. You can contact them at +33 2 31 92 17 00 or visit their website at (https://www.chateau-bellefontaine.com). Another excellent option is the Domaine de Bayeux, located at 20 Rue de Crémel, with rates ranging from €90 to €180 per night. Their contact number is +33 2 31 92 06 45, and their website is (https://www.domaine-de-bayeux.com/en/).

Reaching these parks and picnic spots is straightforward. Parc Michel d'Ornano and the Jardin Public de Bayeux are within walking distance from the town center. The Parc Naturel Régional des Marais du Cotentin et du Bessin can be reached by car, with parking available at various points within the park. Local buses also provide access to some parts of the park, making it accessible even for those without a vehicle.

Chapter 6

Food and Dining

Traditional Norman Cuisine

Norman cuisine is renowned for its rich flavors and use of fresh, local ingredients. The region's culinary traditions are deeply rooted in its agricultural heritage, with a focus on dairy products, apples, seafood, and meats. A visit to Bayeux offers the perfect opportunity to savor these delectable dishes and experience the authentic tastes of Normandy.

One of the most iconic dishes in Norman cuisine is the "Coquilles Saint-Jacques," or scallops. Freshly caught from the nearby English Channel, these scallops are often prepared in a creamy sauce made with butter, cream, and white wine. Another seafood specialty is "Moules à la Normande," mussels cooked with apples, cream, and cider, which highlights the region's famous apple orchards and dairy farms.

Normandy is also famous for its cheeses, with Camembert, Pont-l'Évêque, and Livarot being the most well-known. These cheeses are often enjoyed with a slice of freshly baked bread and a glass of local cider or Calvados, a strong apple brandy that is a staple of the region. "Tarte Tatin," an upside-down caramelized apple tart, is a popular dessert that perfectly encapsulates the region's love for apples.

For those looking to try traditional Norman cuisine in Bayeux, La Rapière is a highly recommended restaurant. Located at 53 Rue Saint-Jean, this charming eatery offers a cozy atmosphere and a menu that showcases the best of Norman flavors.

The average cost per meal is around €30-€50. You can contact La Rapière at +33 2 31 21 05 45 or visit their website at (https://www.larapiere.net/en/).

Top Restaurants and Cafés

Le Pommier is a well-regarded restaurant known for its contemporary take on traditional Norman dishes. The restaurant is located at 40 Rue des Cuisiniers and offers a sophisticated dining experience with a focus on fresh, local ingredients. The average cost per meal is around €35-€60. You can contact Le Pommier at +33 2 31 21 52 10.

For a more casual dining experience, Au Ptit Bistrot is an excellent choice. This cozy bistro offers a relaxed atmosphere and a menu featuring classic French dishes made with local produce. Located at 31 ter rue Larcher 14400 Bayeux France, the average cost per meal at Au Ptit Bistrot is around €20-€35. You can contact them at +33 2 31 92 30 08 or visit (https://www.yelp.com/biz/au-p-tit-bistro-bayeux).

For a unique dining experience, try L'Angle Saint Laurent, which combines French cuisine with a modern twist. Located at 2 Rue des Bouchers, 14400 Bayeux, France, this restaurant offers an elegant setting and a menu that changes with the seasons. The average cost per meal is around €40-€70. You can contact L'Angle Saint Laurent at +33 2 31 92 03 01.

Getting to these restaurants and cafés is straightforward. Most are located in the heart of Bayeux, within walking distance from major attractions such as the Bayeux Cathedral and the Bayeux Tapestry Museum. If you are staying in the town center, you can easily reach them on foot. For those coming from further afield, there are several parking options available nearby, and local buses also provide convenient access.

Food Markets and Local Specialties

Bayeux's food markets are a treasure trove of local specialties, offering visitors the chance to experience the vibrant culinary culture of Normandy. The markets are an excellent place to sample fresh produce, cheeses, meats, and other regional delicacies.

The Bayeux Market, held every Saturday morning at Place Saint-Patrice, is one of the most popular markets in the region. This bustling market features a wide array of stalls selling everything from fresh fruits and vegetables to artisanal cheeses, meats, and baked goods. Visitors can also find local specialties such as Camembert, Pont-l'Évêque, and Livarot cheeses, as well as fresh seafood, charcuterie, and Normandy cider. The market is open from 8:00 AM to 1:00 PM, and it's a must-visit for food enthusiasts.

Another notable market is the Bayeux Organic Market, held every Wednesday afternoon at Place Saint-Patrice. This market focuses on organic and sustainably produced goods, including fresh produce, dairy products, meats, and baked goods. It's an excellent place to find high-quality, organic ingredients and support local farmers and producers. The market operates from 2:00 PM to 6:00 PM.

To reach the Bayeux Market and the Bayeux Organic Market, head to Place Saint-Patrice, which is located in the town center. Both markets are easily accessible on foot from most parts of Bayeux. For those driving, there are several parking options available nearby. If you are taking public transport, local buses stop close to Place Saint-Patrice.

Chapter 7

Shopping in Bayeux

Souvenir Shops

Souvenir shopping in Bayeux is a delightful experience, with numerous shops offering unique and memorable items that capture the essence of the region. These shops provide visitors with a wide range of products, from traditional Norman crafts to items commemorating the town's rich history.

One of the most popular souvenir shops in Bayeux is Boutique Bayeux Tapestry, located at 55 Rue de Nesmond. This shop specializes in products inspired by the famous Bayeux Tapestry, including replicas, books, postcards, and textiles. Prices for souvenirs range from €5 for postcards to €100 for high-quality tapestry replicas. You can contact Boutique Bayeux Tapestry at +33 2 31 92 02 34 or visit their website at (https://www.bayeuxmuseum.com).

Another excellent option is La Boutique Normande, situated at 8 Rue Saint-Martin. This shop offers a variety of traditional Norman products, such as local cider, Calvados, cheeses, and handmade crafts. Prices vary, with items like small bottles of cider costing around €10 and larger gift sets reaching up to €50. You can contact La Boutique Normande at +33 2 31 92 00 77 / +33 2 33 07 41 38.

To reach these souvenir shops, head to the town center, where most of them are conveniently located within walking distance of major attractions like the Bayeux Cathedral and the Bayeux Tapestry Museum. If you're staying in the town center, you can easily explore these shops on foot. For those driving, there are several parking options available nearby. Public transport is also an option, with local buses providing convenient access to the town center.

Local Markets

The Bayeux Market, held every Saturday morning at Place Saint-Patrice, is a must-visit. This vibrant market features a wide array of stalls selling fresh fruits and vegetables, cheeses, meats, baked goods, and other regional delicacies. Prices are generally reasonable, with items like a loaf of bread costing around €2 and a selection of cheeses ranging from €5 to €15. Opening hours for the market are 8:00 AM to 1:00 PM. For more information, you can contact the Bayeux Tourist Office at +33 2 31 51 28 28 or visit their website at (https://www.bayeux-bessin-tourisme.com).

Another notable market is the Bayeux Organic Market, held every Wednesday afternoon at Place Saint-Patrice. This market focuses on organic and sustainably produced goods, including fresh produce, dairy products, meats, and baked goods. It's an excellent place to find high-quality, organic ingredients and support local farmers and producers. The market operates from 2:00 PM to 6:00 PM. For additional details, you can contact the Bayeux Tourist Office at the same number and website provided above.

To reach the Bayeux Market and the Bayeux Organic Market, head to Place Saint-Patrice, located in the town center. Both markets are easily accessible on foot from most parts of Bayeux. If you're driving, there are several parking options available nearby. Public transport is also available, with local buses stopping close to Place Saint-Patrice.

Chapter 8

Day Trips and Excursions

D-Day Landing Beaches

Historical Significance and Overview

The D-Day landing beaches are among the most significant historical sites in the world, marking the location of the Allied invasion of Normandy on June 6, 1944, during World War II. This operation, known as Operation Overlord, was a pivotal moment in the war, leading to the liberation of German-occupied France and eventually all of Western Europe. The invasion involved nearly 156,000 American, British, and Canadian forces landing on five beachheads: Utah, Omaha, Gold, Juno, and Sword.

Utah Beach

Located on the Cotentin Peninsula, Utah Beach was the westernmost of the D-Day beaches. The landing here was relatively successful, with fewer casualties compared to other sites. Today, visitors can explore the Utah Beach Museum, which offers comprehensive exhibits on the planning and execution of the D-Day landings, including personal stories, photographs, and artifacts.

Location: Sainte-Marie-du-Mont, Normandy, France Key Highlights: Utah Beach Museum, D-Day Memorial, preserved German bunkers.

Omaha Beach

Omaha Beach, situated between Sainte-Honorine-des-Pertes and Vierville-sur-Mer, witnessed some of the fiercest fighting on D-Day. The beachhead was critical for establishing a foothold in Normandy, though it came at a great cost. The Normandy American Cemetery and Memorial in Colleville-sur-Mer is a poignant site where thousands of American soldiers are buried. The nearby Overlord Museum offers additional insights into the battle.

Location: Colleville-sur-Mer, Normandy, France
Key Highlights: Normandy American Cemetery, Overlord Museum, Pointe du Hoc.

Gold Beach

Assigned to the British 50th Infantry Division, Gold Beach saw significant battles, particularly around the town of Arromanches. This area is now home to the Arromanches 360 Circular Cinema, which provides a unique audiovisual experience of the D-Day landings. The remnants of the Mulberry Harbors, temporary portable harbors used during the invasion, can still be seen offshore.

Location: Arromanches-les-Bains, Normandy, France
Key Highlights: Arromanches 360 Circular Cinema, Mulberry Harbour remains, D-Day Museum.

Juno Beach

Juno Beach was the landing site for the Canadian 3rd Infantry Division. Despite encountering heavy resistance, the Canadians successfully secured the beach and pushed inland. The Juno Beach Centre in Courseulles-sur-Mer is dedicated to the Canadian troops who fought in Normandy, featuring exhibits on Canada's role in World War II.

Location: Courseulles-sur-Mer, Normandy, France
Key Highlights: Juno Beach Centre, Canadian War Cemetery, preserved Atlantic Wall bunkers.

Sword Beach

Sword Beach, the easternmost landing area, was assigned to the British 3rd Infantry Division. The objective here was to capture the city of Caen, although this goal took longer than expected due to fierce German resistance. Visitors can explore the Pegasus Bridge Museum, which commemorates the airborne landings that supported the Sword Beach assault.

Location: Ouistreham, Normandy, France
Key Highlights: Pegasus Bridge Museum, Hillman Fortress, Atlantic Wall Museum.

Nearby Villages and Towns

Bayeux
Bayeux is not only a gateway to the D-Day beaches but also a charming town with its own rich history. The Bayeux Tapestry, an 11th-century embroidered cloth depicting the Norman Conquest of England, is housed here. The town itself is a delight to explore,

with its medieval architecture, cobbled streets, and the magnificent Bayeux Cathedral.

Key Highlights: Bayeux Tapestry Museum, Bayeux Cathedral, Battle of Normandy Museum.

Sainte-Mère-Église

One of the first towns liberated by Allied forces, Sainte-Mère-Église is famous for the paratrooper John Steele, whose parachute got caught on the church steeple. The Airborne Museum here provides a detailed account of the airborne operations that took place in the early hours of D-Day.

Key Highlights: Airborne Museum, Church of Sainte-Mère-Église, D-Day landmarks.

Honfleur

A picturesque port town, Honfleur is renowned for its old harbor, lined with colorful houses and bustling with activity. It's a wonderful spot to unwind and take in the seaside ambience. The town also has a rich artistic heritage, having inspired many painters, including Claude Monet.

Key Highlights: Vieux Bassin (Old Harbor), Saint-Catherine's Church, Eugène Boudin Museum.

Caen

Caen, a city deeply affected by World War II, is home to the Caen Memorial Museum, which offers a comprehensive overview of the war and the Normandy invasion. The city also boasts historical sites such as the Château de Caen and the Abbaye aux Hommes.

Key Highlights: Caen Memorial Museum, Château de Caen, Abbaye aux Hommes.

Scenic Drives and Tours

La Route des Crêtes

The "Route of the Ridges" offers breathtaking views over the Normandy countryside. This scenic drive takes you through rolling hills, picturesque villages, and lush green landscapes. Key stops along the way include the historic towns of Falaise and Domfront, as well as the stunning Suisse Normande region.

Key Highlights: Falaise Castle, Domfront Old Town, Suisse Normande viewpoints.

Normandy Cider Route

Normandy is famous for its cider, and the Cider Route is a delightful way to explore the region's orchards and cideries. This route winds through the Pays d'Auge, known for its traditional half-timbered houses and apple orchards. Many cider producers offer tours and tastings, providing an authentic taste of Normandy.

Key Highlights: Cider tastings, traditional Norman architecture, picturesque countryside.

Mont Saint-Michel

While a bit further afield, a visit to Mont Saint-Michel is a must when in Normandy. This iconic island commune is one of France's most famous landmarks, with its medieval abbey perched atop a rocky hill. The journey to Mont Saint-Michel offers scenic views of the bay and surrounding landscapes.

Key Highlights: Mont Saint-Michel Abbey, tidal causeway, panoramic views.

The D-Day Route

For those interested in a comprehensive exploration of the D-Day sites, the D-Day Route is an excellent option. This self-guided tour covers all the major beaches, memorials, and museums related to the Normandy invasion. It provides a deep dive into the history of D-Day, allowing visitors to follow in the footsteps of the soldiers who fought there.

Key Highlights: All D-Day beaches, key memorials, and museums, historical insights.

Chapter 9

Cultural Events and Festivals

Annual Festivals and Events

Bayeux, a town rich in history and culture, hosts a variety of annual festivals and events that attract visitors from all over the world. These celebrations offer a unique glimpse into the local traditions and the vibrant community life of this picturesque Norman town. Below are some of the most prominent annual festivals and events in Bayeux.

Bayeux Medieval Festival

The Bayeux Medieval Festival, held every year in July, transforms the town into a medieval wonderland. This event celebrates Bayeux's rich medieval heritage with a series of activities that include jousting tournaments, medieval music performances, artisan markets, and historical reenactments. The festival is a perfect opportunity to experience the town as it would have been in the Middle Ages.

Location: Bayeux Town Center
Website: (https://bayeux-bessin-tourisme.com/en/major-events/the-bayeux-medieval-festival)
Phone Contact: +33 2 31 51 28 28
Getting There: Bayeux can be accessed by train from Paris (Gare Saint-Lazare) to Bayeux station, followed by a short walk to the town center.

Bayeux War Correspondents' Awards

Each October, Bayeux hosts the War Correspondents' Awards, honoring journalists who risk their lives to cover conflicts around the world. This event includes exhibitions, screenings, debates, and the prestigious award ceremony. It's a profound event that emphasizes the importance of journalism and the sacrifices made by war correspondents.

Location: Bayeux Tapestry Museum and various venues
Website: (https://www.prixbayeux.org/en/)
Phone Contact: +33 2 31 92 03 30
Getting There: The Bayeux Tapestry Museum is within walking distance from Bayeux train station.

D-Day Festival

Commemorating the historic D-Day landings, the D-Day Festival is a significant event held in June across the Normandy region, including Bayeux. The festival features parades, reenactments, firework displays, and educational tours of the D-Day landing sites. It is a moving tribute to the bravery and sacrifices of the Allied forces.

Location: Various locations in Bayeux and Normandy

Website: (https://en.normandie-tourisme.fr/partners/d-day-festival-normandy/)

Phone Contact: +33 2 31 51 28 28

Getting There: Various sites can be reached from Bayeux by local transport or guided tours.

Theater and Performances

Bayeux is also home to a vibrant performing arts scene, with several venues hosting a variety of theatrical performances, concerts, and other cultural events throughout the year.

Théâtre Municipal de Bayeux

The Théâtre Municipal de Bayeux is the town's main theater, offering a diverse program of plays, musicals, concerts, and dance performances. The theater aims to promote cultural enrichment and provides a platform for both local and international artists.

Location: 19 Rue Laitière, 14400 Bayeux, France
Website:
(https://www.bayeux.fr/fr/domaine-dactivite/theatre)
Phone Contact: +33 2 31 92 03 30
Getting There: The theater is located in the town center, easily accessible by foot from the train station.

La Halle ô Grains

La Halle ô Grains is another key cultural venue in Bayeux, hosting a range of performances, including contemporary theater, classical music, and dance. The venue is known for its innovative programming and community engagement.

Location: Place aux Pommes, 14400 Bayeux, France
Website: (https://halleograins.bayeux.fr/)
Phone Contact: +33 2 31 92 03 30
Getting There: Centrally located, La Halle ô Grains is within walking distance from most parts of the town.

Local Traditions and Celebrations

Bayeux is a town deeply rooted in tradition, and its local celebrations reflect its rich cultural heritage.

Fête de la Libération

Every August, Bayeux celebrates its liberation from Nazi occupation with the Fête de la Libération. The event includes parades, concerts, and various commemorative ceremonies. It's a time for locals and visitors to honor the memory of those who fought for freedom.

Location: Various locations in Bayeux
Phone Contact: +33 2 31 51 28 28
Getting There: Events are held throughout the town, accessible by foot or local transport.

Fête des Normands

The Fête des Normands is a celebration of Norman culture and identity, held in late September. The festival features traditional Norman music, dance, cuisine, and crafts. It's an excellent opportunity to immerse yourself in the local culture and learn about Norman traditions.

Location: Various locations in Bayeux

Phone Contact: +33 2 31 51 28 28

Getting There: Events are held in various parts of Bayeux, accessible by local transport.

7 Days Itinerary

Day 1: Arrival and Exploration

- Morning: Arrive in Bayeux, check into your hotel, and take a leisurely walk around the town center.
- Afternoon: Visit the Bayeux Tapestry Museum and marvel at the 11th-century embroidery.
- Evening: Enjoy dinner at a local restaurant, such as Le Pommier or La Rapière.

Day 2: Historical Sites

- Morning: Explore the Bayeux Cathedral, a stunning example of Norman architecture.
- Afternoon: Visit the Battle of Normandy Museum to learn about the pivotal events of World War II.
- Evening: Attend a performance at the Théâtre Municipal de Bayeux.

Day 3: D-Day Landing Beaches

- Morning: Take a guided tour to the D-Day landing beaches, starting with Utah Beach and the Utah Beach Museum.
- Afternoon: Continue to Omaha Beach and visit the Normandy American Cemetery.
- Evening: Return to Bayeux and relax at a local café.

Day 4: Local Traditions and Celebrations

- Morning: Participate in the Liberation or Fête des Normands if visiting during these times.

- Afternoon: Stroll through the town's markets and pick up some local produce and crafts.

- Evening: Enjoy a traditional Norman meal and local cider.

Day 5: Nearby Villages and Towns

- Morning: Visit Sainte-Mère-Église and the Airborne Museum.

- Afternoon: Explore the picturesque town of Honfleur, known for its old harbor and artistic heritage.

- Evening: Return to Bayeux and dine at a recommended restaurant.

Day 6: Scenic Drives and Tours

- Morning: Drive along the La Route des Crêtes for stunning views of the Norman countryside.

- Afternoon: Follow the Normandy Cider Route, stopping at various cideries for tastings.

- Evening: Attend a cultural event at La Halle ô Grains.

Day 7: Final Day and Departure

- Morning: Take a final walk through Bayeux, visiting any remaining sites of interest.

- Afternoon: Enjoy a relaxing lunch at a local bistro before preparing for departure.

- Evening: Depart from Bayeux, taking with you memories of a culturally enriching experience.

Chapter 10

Practical Information

Tourist Information Centers

Bayeux Tourist Office

The Bayeux Tourist Office is the main hub for visitor information in the town. It offers a wide range of services, including accommodation bookings, guided tour arrangements, and detailed information about local attractions, events, and transportation.

Location: Pont Saint-Jean, 14400 Bayeux, France
Website: (https://www.bayeux-bessin-tourism.com/en)

Phone Contact: +33 2 31 51 28 28

Hours of Operation: Monday to Saturday, 9:00 AM - 6:00 PM; Sunday and public holidays, 10:00 AM - 5:00 PM

The friendly and knowledgeable staff at the Bayeux Tourist Office can assist with a variety of inquiries, from finding the best restaurants to recommending scenic walking routes. They also provide free maps and brochures to help you navigate the town and its surroundings.

Normandy Tourist Board

For broader information about the Normandy region, the Normandy Tourist Board is an excellent resource. They provide detailed information on regional attractions, events, and accommodations, ensuring that visitors have a comprehensive understanding of what Normandy has to offer.

Website: (https://en.normandie-tourisme.fr/)

Phone Contact: +33 2 31 27 90 30

Bayeux Intercom

Bayeux Intercom is a local inter-municipal organization that offers a range of services to visitors, including information on cultural events, local heritage, and community activities. Their website is a valuable resource for discovering what's happening in and around Bayeux during your visit.

Website: (https://www.bayeux-intercom.fr/)

Phone Contact: +33 2 31 51 63 00

Emergency Contacts

- Police: Dial 17

- Fire Department: Dial 18

- Medical Emergency (SAMU): Dial 15

- European Emergency Number: Dial 112 (can be used for all emergencies)

Hospitals and Medical Services

Centre Hospitalier de Bayeux

The main hospital in Bayeux provides comprehensive medical services, including emergency care.

Location: 13 Boulevard des Fauvelles, 14400 Bayeux, France

Website: (http://www.ch-bayeux.fr/)

Phone Contact: +33 2 31 51 51 51

Pharmacies

Pharmacies are widely available throughout Bayeux. Many offer 24-hour service for urgent medical needs. A list of duty pharmacies (pharmacies de garde) is usually posted on the doors of all pharmacies.

Pharmacie Principale Bayeux

Location: 5 Rue Saint-Malo, 14400 Bayeux, France

Phone Contact: +33 2 31 51 09 45

Travel Tips and Safety Advice

General Safety

Bayeux is a relatively safe town, but it's always important to remain vigilant and take basic precautions:

- Pickpocketing: Pay attention to your surroundings, particularly in populated places. Preserve your possessions and refrain from putting expensive things on show.

- Emergency Contacts: Always have the local emergency numbers (listed above) handy.

- Local Laws and Customs: Respect local laws and customs. Familiarize yourself with French regulations regarding public behavior, drinking, and smoking.

Accommodation

Bayeux offers a variety of accommodation options, from luxury hotels to budget-friendly hostels. Try making reservations in advance, particularly during the busiest travel times. Websites like (https://www.booking.com/)and(https://www.expedia.com/) can help you find suitable accommodations.

Visa Requirement and Permit

Schengen Visa for EU and EEA Citizens

Citizens of the European Union (EU) and European Economic Area (EEA) do not require a visa to enter France. They can travel freely to Bayeux and other parts of France using their national identification card or passport.

Schengen Visa for Non-EU Citizens

Non-EU citizens from visa-exempt countries can enter France for short stays (up to 90 days within a 180-day period) without a visa. This includes nationals from countries like the United States, Canada, Australia, and Japan. A visa is needed for additional purposes or for longer stays.

Visa Types:

- Short-Stay Visa (Schengen Visa): Allows stays up to 90 days for tourism, business, or family visits.
- Long-Stay Visa: Required for stays longer than 90 days, such as for study, work, or residence.

Application Process:

1. Determine Visa Type: Identify the type of visa required for your stay.
2. Complete Application Form: Fill out the appropriate visa application form.
3. Gather Required Documents: Typically includes a valid passport, recent passport-sized photos, travel

itinerary, proof of accommodation, travel insurance, and proof of financial means.

4. Submit Application: Submit the application and required documents to the French consulate or embassy in your home country. Some countries may allow online submission through platforms like (https://france-visas.gouv.fr/).

5. Attend Appointment: Attend a visa appointment at the consulate or visa application center, if required.

Website: (https://france-visas.gouv.fr/)

Work and Study Permits

- Work Permit: Obtainable through your employer or sponsoring organization.

- Study Permit: Required for international students enrolling in French educational institutions. Usually, you need an acceptance letter from the institution.

Website: (https://www.campusfrance.org/en)

Other Permits

- Residence Permit: For those planning to stay in France for an extended period (more than 90 days).
- Family Reunification Permit: For family members of EU/EEA nationals residing in France.

Conclusion

As you've journeyed through this travel guide, you've discovered the many facets that make Bayeux a must-visit destination. Its architectural marvels, such as the magnificent Notre-Dame Cathedral and the meticulously preserved medieval streets, provide a picturesque backdrop that transports visitors back in time. The town's museums and galleries, including the Musée de la Tapisserie and the Baron Gérard Museum of Art and History, offer deep insights into the art, culture, and heritage of Bayeux.

Bayeux is not just a place of historical significance but also a hub of cultural vitality. The town celebrates everything from modern art to medieval history with a plethora of festivals and events held all year long. The bustling markets, cozy cafes, and gourmet restaurants offer a taste of Normandy's renowned culinary delights, while the friendly locals add a personal touch to every interaction, making visitors feel at home.

For those seeking to explore beyond the town's borders, Bayeux serves as an excellent base for day trips and excursions. The nearby D-Day landing beaches and memorials provide a poignant reminder of the sacrifices made during World War II. Charming villages like Arromanches and Port-en-Bessin, as well as scenic drives through the Normandy countryside, offer additional layers of beauty and exploration.

Practical information included in this guide ensures that you are well-prepared for your visit. From navigating the town with the help of tourist information centers to understanding visa requirements and emergency contacts, every detail has been covered to make your trip smooth and enjoyable. Travel tips and safety advice further enhance your ability to experience Bayeux with confidence and ease.

As you plan your itinerary, the suggested seven-day plan provides a comprehensive and balanced approach to experiencing the best of Bayeux and its surroundings. Each day has been thoughtfully crafted to ensure you don't miss any of the highlights, while still allowing for the flexibility to explore at your own pace. Safe travels, and enjoy the enchanting town of Bayeux!

Bonus

Would You Rather Family Game Question for your Relaxation and Family Time out

Would You Rather Questions for Adults

_1._

Would you rather visit a new city every year or relax at the same beach resort every year?

_2._

Would you rather have an all-expenses-paid vacation to anywhere in the world or receive $5,000 in cash?

_3._

Would you rather go on a romantic cruise or a thrilling safari?

_4._

Would you rather travel to a remote island or a bustling metropolitan city?

5.

Would you rather explore ancient ruins or discover modern architecture?

6.

Would you rather eat only local cuisine on vacation or have the option for familiar fast food?

7.

Would you rather stay in a luxurious hotel or a cozy bed and breakfast?

8.

Would you rather have a quiet vacation in a small village or an adventurous trip in a big city?

9.

Would you rather travel with your family or take a solo trip?

10.

Would you rather have a relaxing spa day or an action-packed adventure day?

11.

Would you rather visit a famous landmark or a hidden gem?

12.

Would you rather spend your vacation hiking in the mountains or swimming in the ocean?

13.

Would you rather have perfect weather on your vacation or perfect company?

14.

Would you rather take a road trip across your country or fly to a foreign land?

15.

Would you rather have unlimited flight tickets or never have to pay for accommodation again?

16.

Would you rather visit every country in Europe or every state in the USA?

17.

Would you rather have a vacation planned by a professional or plan it yourself?

18.

Would you rather have a vacation where you can only take pictures or only make videos?

19.

Would you rather visit a national park or an amusement park?

20.

Would you rather go on a guided tour or explore on your own?

21.

Would you rather have a vacation filled with adventure or one filled with relaxation?

22.

Would you rather travel by train or by ship?

23.

Would you rather have a technology-free vacation or a luxury tech-savvy vacation?

24.

Would you rather visit the hottest or the coldest place on Earth?

25.

Would you rather have a vacation full of surprises or one that is completely predictable?

26.

Would you rather have a year-long vacation in one place or travel to 12 different places in a year?

27.

Would you rather visit a place where you don't speak the language or travel somewhere that feels just like home?

28.

Would you rather travel back in time to a historical event or travel forward in time to see the future?

29.

Would you rather have a vacation with unlimited gourmet food or unlimited entertainment?

30.

Would you rather visit a destination with a rich cultural history or a place known for its natural beauty?

31.

Would you rather have a vacation with all your friends or one with just your partner?

32.

Would you rather spend your vacation budget on experiences or souvenirs?

33.

Would you rather visit a famous museum or attend a local festival?

34.

Would you rather have a vacation where you are constantly active or one where you can relax most of the time?

35.

Would you rather travel to a new place every month or have one extended trip each year?

36.

Would you rather travel somewhere new or return to your favorite destination?

37.

Would you rather have a beach vacation or a mountain retreat?

38.

Would you rather have a vacation in a camper van or stay in luxury resorts?

39.

Would you rather visit a famous tourist spot or a little-known local favorite?

40.

Would you rather have a vacation with no plans at all or one with a detailed itinerary?

41.

Would you rather travel for the food or for the sights?

42.

Would you rather have unlimited money for shopping or for activities on your vacation?

43.

Would you rather have a vacation where you learn a new skill or one where you do nothing at all?

44.

Would you rather have a vacation that's nonstop busy or one with lots of downtime?

45.

Would you rather take a relaxing hot air balloon ride or go skydiving?

46.

Would you rather have a vacation in a place with amazing nightlife or one with breathtaking natural scenery?

47.

Would you rather travel during the busy tourist season or the quiet off-season?

48.

Would you rather visit a place with a rich history or one known for its modern attractions?

49.

Would you rather stay in a place with no internet or no hot water?

50.

Would you rather have a surprise vacation planned by someone else or plan every detail yourself?

Would You Rather Questions for Kids

1.

Would you rather visit Disneyland or go on a safari?

2.

Would you rather eat ice cream every day on vacation or get a new toy every day?

3.

Would you rather go to the beach or go to a water park?

4.

Would you rather visit a zoo or an aquarium?

5.

Would you rather go camping in the woods or stay in a fancy hotel?

6.

Would you rather have a day full of rides at an amusement park or a day full of games at an arcade?

7.

Would you rather meet your favorite cartoon character or your favorite animal?

8.

Would you rather ride a horse or a camel?

9.

Would you rather swim with dolphins or go whale watching?

10.

Would you rather go to a tropical island or a snowy mountain?

11.
Would you rather have unlimited candy on vacation or unlimited pizza?

12.
Would you rather visit a dinosaur museum or a space museum?

13.
Would you rather have a vacation with lots of sports or lots of arts and crafts?

14.
Would you rather fly on an airplane or ride on a train?

15.

Would you rather visit a farm or a castle?

16.
Would you rather go on a treasure hunt or a scavenger hunt?

17.
Would you rather have a vacation with no homework or one with lots of new books to read?

18.
Would you rather stay in a treehouse or a castle?

19.
Would you rather go to a magic show or a circus?

20.
Would you rather visit a jungle or a desert?

21.

Would you rather go to a birthday party every day or a sleepover every night?

22.
Would you rather have a vacation where you can play with animals or one where you can play video games?

23.
Would you rather go on a pirate ship or a spaceship?

24.
Would you rather visit a place where it's always sunny or always snowy?

25.
Would you rather eat breakfast with your favorite superhero or dinner with your favorite princess?

26.

Would you rather have a vacation full of surprises or one where you know everything in advance?

27.

Would you rather go on a roller coaster or a Ferris wheel?

28.

Would you rather visit a place with lots of history or lots of modern attractions?

29.

Would you rather have a vacation with lots of sports or one with lots of arts and crafts?

30.

Would you rather go on a nature hike or visit a science museum?

31.

Would you rather have a vacation where you see lots of animals or lots of toys?

32.

Would you rather visit a theme park or a national park?

33.

Would you rather have a vacation with lots of water activities or lots of land activities?

34.

Would you rather visit a place with lots of different foods to try or one with lots of different games to play?

35.

Would you rather go to a carnival or a fair?

36.

Would you rather have a vacation where you can ride bikes or one where you can ride horses?

37.

Would you rather visit a place with lots of puzzles or lots of playgrounds?

38.

Would you rather have a vacation with lots of music or lots of movies?

39.

Would you rather take a boat ride or a rail ride?

40.

Would you rather have a vacation with lots of swimming or lots of hiking?

41.

Would you rather prefer to see a little town or a large city?

42.

Would you rather have a vacation with lots of exploring or lots of relaxing?

43.

Would you rather visit a famous landmark or a hidden gem?

44.

Would you rather go to a place with lots of nature or lots of buildings?

45.

Would you rather have a vacation with lots of sports or lots of arts and crafts?

46.

Would you rather visit a place with lots of animals or lots of toys?

47.

Would you rather go to a magic show or a circus?

48.

Would you rather visit a place where you can play in the sand or play in the snow?

49.

Would you rather have a vacation with lots of friends or lots of family?

50. Would you rather visit a place with lots of water activities or lots of land activities?

Printed in Great Britain
by Amazon